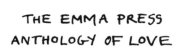

THE EMMA PRESS
ANTHOLOGY OF LOVE

THE EMMA PRESS
ANTHOLOGY OF LOVE

Edited by Rachel Piercey and Emma Wright

Illustrated by Emma Wright

THE EMMA PRESS

THE EMMA PRESS

First published in Great Britain in 2018 by the Emma Press Ltd

Poems copyright © individual copyright holders 2018
Selection copyright © Rachel Piercey and Emma Wright 2018
Illustrations copyright © Emma Wright 2018

ISBN 978-1-910139-56-1

A CIP catalogue record of this book
is available from the British Library.

Printed and bound in Great Britain
by TJ International, Padstow.

The Emma Press
theemmapress.com
queries@theemmapress.com
Jewellery Quarter, Birmingham, UK

CONTENTS

When are you coming for coffee?

grand and easy, easy and grand

that sharp tang

my swaying ear of corn

breathe out ghosts

Let's both

THE EMMA PRESS
ANTHOLOGY OF LOVE

Not quite déjà vu

Ascending the water ride
I suddenly remember Leith,
the four of us pissed and maudlin,
conversation fading into sleep
until Alec drains his glass,
tells Maude she's all that matters,
his cheeks flushed as an open heart
and you say 'You're so lucky'
then stop, look away before I understand.
Sometimes memories make circles,
glint like birds in the light;
plummeting now, eyes blurred,
I think of your face,
how my stomach lurched.

Falooda

I have a friend who always believed
love was like being touched
by a livewire or swimming

on her back in a lightning storm.
I want to tell her it's homesickness,
how longing pulls us in funny ways.

We go walking through
all the rooms of our lives
eating cold sweet things:

saffron ices, rose syrup and milk
in a tall glass, Persian cucumber ice cream
light as muslin. Such gentle

gods say be still and listen. They say
how love is a greenwood that deepens,
how every desert hides a well.

Green Blue Yellow

on the hottest of days
lay down on likewedid the grass
and listen to likewedid poetry
with me:

don't get up and I won't either

there is a sky as blue as gas rings
as cartoon dolphins
which is invisible to us

we are busy silently listening

your eyelids are full of happy gold
my eyelids are full of sad gold

Romantic

It's hard to mourn in shorts, a straw hat, flip-flops.
Cats from the sanctuary sunbathe nude
on the headstones, or cool the embassies
of themselves among the pomegranate trees.

Would the cicadas ever quit buckling their ribs.
A gecko goes bouldering over Antonio Gramsci's grave
and the beautiful teeth of American tourists are sparkling
but they can't help it, and we are tourists too.

We drink water by the jeroboam
and go over again the terrible things Percy Shelley did
in the name of his fireproof heart.
Die by drowning or don't – these remain our options.

The water cycle magics on like something
finer than a clock and John Keats
it's nice to meet you, under the circumstances.
And John Keats, please excuse us, time has made it late.

It's today already
and we have only the rest of our lives.
Long may we dabble our feet in the clear Italian lakes.
Long may we mosey through the graveyards of the world.

When are you coming for coffee?

Yes

Boy at the off licence,
you are slightly too old for this job
and you are not beautiful.

But you hold my eye

so I say 'Yes'
to the taster of pink fizz

refused by the sensible women
('working' 'driving' 'kids')
ahead of me in the queue.

It is 11am on Sunday
and you look like you know
the way out of the weight of the world.

So yes, I will run away with you

at least as far
as the bins round the back
with the rest of the bottle.

Dear Lab-Man

Yesterday I wrote your name on a single cell,
engraved split hearts on algae. I broke the rules,
left a lipstick mark on a Petri dish. Each day
I watch you tend to pipettes dripping
like your children's noses. I speak to you
in elemental signs: here are pearls of mercury
for your wife. I dissect your echoes, the chaos
of your coat — drawn to a fission of dark
I collect laces of damaged DNA, each molecule
a coded rom-com, a self-contained flame,
inside each flame a thousand fireworks.
There's no excuse for my welling up,
strangling all that tubing to spell out LOVE.
My lips can distil blood, meet me
at the fume cupboard tonight.

Perfect Afternoon

It's freezing out.

All the inside tables are taken
and all the outside tables are free.

You sit down.

The waiter sees you
and looks away.

He doesn't want to be outside
and you aren't dressed like big tippers.

You sit there,
not really waiting,
you in love with her
and she in love with you.

I Cannot Name Your Birds

I call them all starlings because they are yours
and because love is   this naming this
oh you are precious   you ruffled and seeking
star-speckled   stay
in this word I have brought it   *starling*
live here   where I know
          how to find you

To the Hairs On My Lover's Back

You've always had these
tiny hairs – here – between

your shoulder blades
– women are deciduous –

but in this heat-wave
the sun has turned them

      golden
            so that

standing there
      in this evening

cooking dinner
      in your underwear

you resemble sunshine
– have assumed something of its nature

as people do
who spend each day together –

but also
      rain – yes

the way a tree's branches
under streetlight

seem to spiral

              inwards

towards the lit
radiating centre –

the way rainwater
caressing branches

        ignites

Note from Edinburgh

Ten years on, I've learnt to wake up
to the light of streetlamps

and a locked moon.
The city breathes out

hot steam from paper cups,
burnt wood, the sound of sourdough

in paper-bags,
and from the swimming pool –

the heat of peppermint and chlorine,
the sweat of water.

I've learned the lake's frost spines,
how water turns

to silence,
the way the leaves of almost-yellow almost

cover the ground.
Look,

I'm making coffee-plum biscotti,
Limoncello cake, amaretto

pears, dark chocolate meringues
and this is only

breakfast.
Winter makes me hungry

but it's not
because of that.

When are you coming for coffee?

Today and Tomorrow

Today, of all your days, you might decide
to certify that you are happy,
by which I mean you woke beside
some gentle other, dreamlike. Not too sappy,
I guess, to say
that every casual sight seems swarming
with sudden zest, a sway
you fall in step with, feeling new attachment forming?

Tomorrow, you're aware, awaits and may be less
uplifting, more
the old defeat. Yet what's in store
you're energised to meet with open arms
because, though metros roar and troubles roll, love's mess
has shown its true serene.
Now all alarms
fall silent. Life renews. Far hills are stippled green.

Yes, it's high time to stir and look alive.
Daredevil hoverflies converge
on motley light. Clumped thistles thrive,
expulsing purplish petals. Here the surge
of rompered spring
is on the breeze and in the hedge,
insistent: 'Anything
can happen.' Unselfconscious, songbirds start to fledge.

You feel perhaps you are, of all those ever born,
        the most impelled
        by love, how all its liftings meld
    and concentrate belief toward a point
and how that feeling spreads like wind through endless corn,
        which guides the spirit on
            till out of joint
with Earth at first, but then—most present when it's gone.

Sending Love

1 Corinthians 13: version 2

You've many hearts but not mine, valentine.
My love is not a valentine—
my love

speeds like the tongues of angels when there's signal;
when answerphones and end-call symbols
can't get through to love

love looks again and spies you in the crowd,
talks past barriers until allowed
to love

burns, I suppose, a little like a rose:
once read it opens as it grows
in love

is ancient, blind, untrendily
hopeful what the end will be
for love

cannot be glued and fails to be self-sticking:
this stamp's a puny substitute for kissing
your lips my love

like shellfish, but that won't go in the post:
oysters must wait until you're close
enough to love

improperly, to rise up unprovoked,
to print your skin with stronger strokes:
LOVE

a childish thing, glow-in-the-dark,
a small and stubborn, ever-fixèd mark,
this love

hides in the pen and letter's crease,
trying to last past letters' cease—
with love
hopefully enclosed,
x

Luigi

You weren't the obvious choice;
muted,
not like your brother –
red-breasted
as a Coca Cola Santa.

You were green.
Tall and slender
as a poplar.

Your leaps
ungainly, shy,
a moustachioed Bambi
all knee,
all prominent rib.

You caught my eye like a feather
from the air.

You grew to twice
your former size
under my hot-water gaze.

Little brother.

Your plumber's hands
your handful of wrench
your eyes
our love
mushrooming in the shadow.

PAULIUS NORVILA

Poem

and the fact we're sitting together at the same table
doesn't mean anything yet,
that we're sharing water, bread,
newspapers and
that we forgive each other's mistakes,
that we understand
what happened, even without words.

it also doesn't mean anything
that we become equal for a moment,
shoulder to shoulder
sticking our fingers
into the dwindling fire of discussion.

it doesn't mean anything,
because maybe we don't know each other at all
and just coincidences brought us together,
ones we don't want to remember right now.

*

it doesn't mean anything.

and if it means something,
then just to those
who never got to
sit next to us

and now near the door
they show their tongues resentfully.

TRANSLATED BY JAYDE WILL

green socks in april

in the snow in april at fifty five and three quarters
she arrived at her wedding wearing a red skirt and
green socks in a battered black sports car called mavis.

she smilingly greeted her beloved and his brightly
checked shirt, galloped to the ladies' room, dumped
the stomach-clenching magic knickers in the sanitary
disposal bin, and strode out ready to breathe
into the serious business of getting married.

afterwards they pulled up in a car park, had a cuddle and
a kiss and a bleary eyed *we're married – wow!* moment,
ambled to the washrooms, changed into long johns and
woolly jumpers, watered off old debris from their hands,
smiled at shiny new rings, and ran from the blow-dryer
back to the plumpness of each other's arms.

Louder Than Words

He made fifteen cups of tea in one morning.
Each time he offered she said yes.
And so he'd retreat to the well-worn kitchen,
to the limp-limbed mug tree,
the toiling kettle;
place her empty cup on the side.

She drank fifteen cups of tea that morning
because love infused the gesture;
while his tired exhalations mingled with the steam,
the martyred milk completed the gift.
If he offered one hundred thousand teas,
each time she would say yes please.

grand and easy, easy and grand

sorry (i forgot your Unbirthday) e e

I like the way our bodies go
together as gelato. How my dark arm
is against your tummy, a swirl in dawn.
In that gentle spoon. The wonga vine
of your hair, black blossom in my face.
I could breathe all of you in. My lips
settle in places on your spine, or fall
away to find new things, although they've
been there, again and again. I like the night.
Its dreamy convalescence, your daggy
chequered pyjamas, my teeth
undoing the drawstring of everything.

Letter composed to Ghengis Khan in my head (whilst in bed)

It's been said that you
fathered hundreds to different
wives in many beds but
did this make you joyous?
I ponder this as I try to sleep
pushed to the edge
of the mattress with my infant
son taking up the space I'm meant
to sleep in. I have read that half
of Asia can trace lineage to you.
Did this make your life worthwhile?
I don't know. I do think though that
I'm more than happy in this
single double
bed with
this one
wife, this
only progeny.

As I Did The Night Before

It was the way you used to put your tights on,
after a moment of loving
        or at the dawn of a new morning.
There was nothing more sensual
        or visual
than you sitting at the edge of the bed
taking your tights in your hands;
softly, tenderly and gently
lost in that moment of intimacy.

And you'd begin
with one leg folded into your body
and your foot pointed elegantly;
you would unroll a film of nylon
that would sheathe and cling
over tips of toes,
ball and sole,
arch and ankle,
over stubborn heel,
sailing steadily
up the calf of an extended leg.
A ritual so beautiful
it had to be repeated.

And when completed
with both feet on the ground
you would rise,
gracefully poised as a ballerina
at the barre;

bending at the waist with legs straight,
you would unroll the rest of your garment
with sweet dexterity
across knees and up golden thighs
until they finally ascended
over a round delicate derrière
where waist bands settle
and gussets reach at the meeting of your thighs.

And you stood tiptoe to ensure that all was covered,
body stretched and arched for a moment.
You held that pose.

Finally, with an encore,
you would bend over one more time,
caressing and smoothing out
unsightly folds or ripples that you found
      as I did the night before
when we had reached our pinnacle.

I held you tenderly and lovingly,
smoothing out the swell and tide
that still lingered in the bodies
of two lovers overwhelmed in love.

Paul

Let me take an inventory. Your brogue, as soft
as Donegal tweed. Your luxuriant hair, fed daily
with potions shipped from overseas. Each tuft
of your groomed eyebrows. Your buying presents early
for remembered birthdays. Not least, the fact
you're short and square. The way you giggle when
excited, and hug your elbows. Your tact.
In hotels, your ringing room service for an iron.
Your love of miniatures and boxes. Your distrust
of all pretence. The way you're followed by
both dogs around the house. Your becoming obsessed
with things you want to buy – a painting, say,
or a cashmere sweater. Your body's warmth at night
when we lie skin to skin. The way it feels right.

Over the Fence

'Aye, a na, he is a pig
but he's also a king as well
with grand argyll wings
and eyes like a canny harlequin,
makin me laugh,
and mesmerising my interiors.
All lies, a na,
but butter-softened,
sweet and tasty
on the tip of me tongue, even
when it's acid-spittin.

Aye, a na, a na,

he's won
but his sugar postpartum
is worth a king's ransom
n any argyll leathers he fancies havin.
N look at him,
he's handsome.'

JANE BURN

Higgedy-Piggedy, my fair hen

I sing to my sweet-bird, sweet-heart, sweet-nest,
sweet-breast, sweet-stomach down on our ovalled
young. Sometimes nine, sometimes ten, our happy
omens in albumen. Little tick-tick of forming yolks,
snug in a calcium spot-skin of fragile wall. Tail-grow,
leg-grow, lung-grow, head-grow – all the while,
my gull-wife's lullaby croon. Grow calm, grow
good, grow lovely in your orby traps. Turn them,
turn them tadpoles, eating up the yellow gold.

Eat yourself, my petrel-Queen, I tell to the urchin
of mine eyes. I will sit thee time enough to swag
your creamy crop with gullet-fish, gizzard-silver,
slip down, lovely codlings. Take the sky, re-open
yourself to the salt air, bring back a nursery rhyme
for our chicklings' new-formed ears. Chant them,
spell them into being – soak the knowing of oceans
through them shells. Come back to me – our love
is an albatross. It will not bear halving.

Our clutch with its bare grip on cliff is woken,
faddling with egg-tooth on husk – the time will soon
be now. What falls from this sheer will be mourned.
What lives will be fed on belly's silt. She is back,
my fallen star – we beak our needs, clatter to swear
fidelity again. She preens and dips her bullet head.
I swap my place with her and she feathers down.
My voice is the scrape of rock on rock to the world
but to her, the ecstasy of togetherness, joy of us.

The Harvest

I want to marry you on harvest morning
when damp presses against windows
and spiders lie flat out in thread houses.

In this little church beneath rocks,
beneath sky, beneath God,
the world smells like the earth that it is.

All our futures unravel here,
where harvest gifts lean up to flowers
and sunlight stacks on a plaited loaf.

The years will drop away, unnoticed,
until we lie in state on worn sofas,
old age sleeping on us

as the shadows sag down the walls
through the hours of a weekday afternoon.
Pergolesi will be even more fragile,

you'll still be insisting you're a memorialist,
I'll still be dreaming up lines about you
and making the tea will be an event.

But we will always be the same under older,
    kinder, skin.

Fifth February, 1983

In cold FebRuary,
only us, our wItnesses
Joan and Colin,
and Joan's boyfriend wHo
just cAme along
foR the hell of it.

A strange Day.

After the cereMony
a classy Bucks Fizz at our local whilE you,
romantic, sLipped off to the Post Office,
the brown enVelope of the pay roll
couldn't be forgotten just because of our weddIng day.
Then to Tate GalLery, not Upton Park as you suggested,
with a Greek mezze and rivers of BeaujoLais at night.
I was clad in grEen to tilt at bad luck.

Lemman

Lover, slumberjack, roll over in
your clown pyjamas, wonder if
it's really all from here true comfort comes –

from ticket stubs and hotel breakfast deals,
and cooking meals together. Chop for you,
and save what's left the way you ask me to,

and stock the fridge for you with juice, lemon
parfait, two kinds of cheese with unfamiliar names,
salmon for bagels. Share a single plate.

The little rituals I assimilate,
like washing rice, wearing more red
and sleeping on just one side of the bed

(though sometimes, your first night away,
on yours). So find me in the kitchen
where I'll kiss your neck and whisper

in your ear how I like the way you
dislike things more than I like
the way most people like the things they like,

and feel like this could be the future,
leaning lightly on your shoulder, cracking jokes
about your thermal-stockinged legs.

I can't believe the way you poach those eggs.

Valentine

The dog, tongue out, and bum down almost flat,
sits waiting for its owner to release
it from the railing she has leashed
it to, to go and buy a this or that.
The dog strains at its collar, starts to whine,
Why is my mummy taking so much time?

And barely missing poor dog on the floor,
a little girl, on scooter, flashes past.
Her father frowns and, thinking she's too fast,
quickens his pace and grabs her at the corner.
He only wants her to slow down and stay
the little girl she is now one more day.

And coming to this turn just by the shop,
a postman in his van, who's seen the girl
and been reminded others share his world,
reduces speed, then finds a gentle stop,
exits, and swings his sack onto his back,
inside of which are letters, cards and packets

all addressed to those who live within
these streets that me and you happen to dwell
in too. The postman checks, then rings the bell
and hands to you, my darling wife, a gift
that sings just like the blue tit in the yew
outside our kitchen window: I love you.

Larder

In case this harvest doesn't last, I'll set something by:
fire a drum of applewood to smoke split kisses;
fillet laughter, pack it into pots with oil and herbs.
I'll seal your voice in shiny tins, string private jokes
and dry them, press a bunch of your best anecdotes.

Your hangovers will feed the compost heap, along
with crossness when I come home late, flu-induced
self-pity, a taste for horror films. And I'll throw on
football absences and Leonard Cohen times.

But against the day the cornucopia runs out,
I'll have a hoard: memories of Norway layered in salt;
whispers distilled in tiny bottles; vacuum-packs
of secret looks; nights simmered in honeydew, poured
into jars and stored where the sun shines through.

Requited

This, then, is love
(at least for you and me)
:
the waves soothing
the sweating brow of the land;
the wet-glass sand
smoothing the nightsheets
of the sea.

The Record Player

for Marie

We brought the record player home
like it was a great prize. I had never owned one
and music in our small bed-sit
was a repeated miracle all that summer.
Everything shone. The future was more possible
than the past. Breathless. I was a pot bubbling over.
Do you remember?

Just out of uni, working, money so new
and exciting. The things you could do with it.
If you pared it down and saved the shavings,
the things you could turn it into.

Do you remember the way we talked,
the way each moment was bright
when we turned it over, the discoveries we made?
Walking down those steps between high fences
to come, at a corner, on open water
stretching its dazzle at the edge of the city,
hidden behind houses. Wasn't that how it was?

I see you stopped in the doorway
of our home in Dubai, after I've hunted out
one of those old tunes, and watch it take you
by surprise, your face young with delight.

And isn't that how it should be for us now –
grand and easy, easy and grand?

that sharp tang

My First Husband

Smith. Impossible
to google
what you're up to now,

miles away, or dead
perhaps. My wedding ring
was a cowrie shell

borrowed from Mrs Bell's Object Box.
You said we'd never give it back.
A traditional match – you

with your car and trucks, me
in the Wendy house,
too wrapped up

with Tiny Tears
to question much. You had affairs,
so did I, it was the Sixties

after all. We lasted five years,
half a lifetime. *Sugar, Sugar*
was our song. Cherry cola, two straws,

at the Leavers' Disco.
I moved house,

we didn't stay in touch.

But in the rearview mirror
I glanced
twice

at the man with thinning hair
who pulled into the parking bay
at Sainsbury's

when I drove off
to pick the children up from school.

First Kiss

The first time anyone kissed me
and, yes, it was like that;
he knew what he was doing
and I did not, though I'd practised
on the bathroom mirror
and on my pillow case
and on the back of my arm.

Anyway, that first time
I jumped at the chance
of the real thing. Valentine's Day
and no cards for me,
they were for the girls
with the back-combed hair,
Janet Tansley and June Smith.

So when Mick and Jim
sent a message to the girls
in the needlework room
at lunch-time, I got up
and went. I fancied Jim
but it was Mick I kissed first,
all brilliantine and swagger,

and he knew how to kiss
but the best of it was
the trembling. Afterwards
it was like a pact, something
new had been spoken.
I moved on to Jim,
a woman and he knew it.

I am not One of Those People

who forget about their friends
when they fall in love, oh no!
I call them one by one
so they may know
that I met a man
who makes his own pizza dough,
clearly a mad man,
because who makes pizza from scratch
when you can just order in,
a man who owns a rolling pin
and knows how to use it,
who talks about glaciers, Klezmer, the Book of Kells,
a man with beautiful hands and prominent clavicles,
with eyes the colour of the Greenland ice sheet
under the rising moon.

ANJA KONIG

I Wake At 6am

The birds are at it already
broadcasting urgently.
It's nearly spring.
I am listening in:
the light in his eyes!
says the blackbird,
his serious soul! its flint of wit!
sings the titmouse,
his hair the colour of steel!
his hip bones, his knees!
natter the sparrows.
A warbler agrees. The birds
are speaking of you, I see.
Outside the light deepens
from blush to bright.

On Opening a Love Note Delivered by Snail

I might just be a simple mushroom, bruised by weathers
and tipped by gloom, but you're one too (though far more moon-like).
I've heard you pulse your hyphae-strings many times,
tripping out a melody for my 'shroomy ears to hear.
I sang back every night to your fruiting body, gills rippling.
You've been eyeing me too, lifting up your pearl skirt
a little further each day, you flirt.

You don't belong in that distant dirt. Look over this deciduous lap
and see – I'm dipping my cap to you. It's taken me two weeks
to twist my stem down and around –
I'm sponge, and open to any crushing boot to stamp your way.
I'd choose to be the one to break in two,
if it gave you an extra day.

And listen, if we *both* move, migrate, we can start our patch
in half the time! Picture the young spores we'll have –
little meteorites, throbbing mycelium love notes like stars
to illuminate our wilting days. They might inherit your egg-shine,
or the convex of my cap. They'll bulb up, all clean, and we'll rub
up the cusps of each other until we stick, blunting memory-smudges
of where we've been, the underneaths only we've seen, all raw ribs.

I can't wait to metabolise matter with you, consume a legume or two.
We can be casual at first, bloom, and then shrink under tented matters
as we feed our buttoned galley, *the family*.
I get softer with age, so be tender with me. I take in the sun
through a skinless skull – so consider this sensitivity when you respond.
For us the earth is quick, and we won't be standing here long.
Send the messenger snail back forthwith, with your answer –
he's not the quickest, you know,
and for us time is of the essence.

Gâteau St Honoré in a Guernsey Hotel

'And for the young lady?' the waiter asked father
in the hotel dining room so I'd chosen the Coke,
the bottle chilled, opened and half poured
with the elegance meted out to mother's Dubonnet –
bitter lemon swirling into pomegranate red over ice,
a lemon slice balanced on the rim –
'And a straw for the *young lady*,' she'd said.
And we had both smiled,

me still floating on air, barely landed from the flight,
from you and that sharp tang that was first love,
then the first taste of fizzing red, father ordering the dessert trolley,
the pastry crown appearing, honey-coloured,
cream-filled bubbles smeared thickly with glossy caramel
consumed blissfully, slowly against their silence.

my swaying ear of corn

Sheanimal

bed me in the dark ferns, soft earth
pebbles touch me hard

I have heard the clamour of nightfall birds
they are calling to you
I have seen the river toss in its bed
and shake for want of you

midges hover in their clouds
of hot silk shaking
above the crowded plants
we snap our jaws at them
rain, we will bring it
nest, burrow
we will and go
at our leisure

my teeth snapped that spine
I thought only of you darling
you darling my you
you will lick the blood off of me

tonight I sleep near you
come running thru deep puddles with me
in the morning after rain
shake dry with me

praise – ground that holds you up
praise – day your mother howled you out
praise – every water gulp you
praise – flies on your pelt
praise – fuck

Postscript

What if love's not well-tooled keys and locks, glass slippers, or mutilated feet?
What if love's like tracing a silhouette in a peasouper

or like watching Polaroid paper etch itself with shades? In the slow furrow
of the nightshift hours, when workers – returning or leaving –

bruise at the edges, nod themselves back into sleep, love might keep schtum,
might speak in whiskers and bristles, jowls, spiney hair,

an awesome stink. O my godmother: for a woman to play low-stakes poker
with her friends is not, in my view, the least bit shocking.

Neither are these things call for alarm: excessive literature consumption;
making the first move. We have fallen

asleep on the back step, chins in claws, feet tucked snug, while the universe
is bearing down its icy helmet of stars.

He shifts and settles again, cranking out snore and purr, dreaming acetate reels.
How is it September already? I go inside; I leave the kitchen door adrift.

The Noonday Devil

I wept my way down from you
to life alone again.

Long before we met I'd yearned
for our knees to mingle.
You thought of light and *were* light,
made it look so damn easy.

I thought of wanting light
so you left me wanting. I rewrote my part:
deaf child at wedding party
holding the six of spades.
Cast you as the groom that got away.

Speaking of black, I saw my mind today
hovering like a bag of wasps
over a wannabe Californian Jesus.
It's a one-track mind with a two-bit agenda
in a world where only three things are certain:
mirth, melancholy and loose change
(seems there's always something I need change for –
the four dollar shoes, the week with five Fridays).

There was another after you. The noonday devil.
He sucked with his face down. Christ, he felt good
but I have no heart for a man
who can go a week without reading.
Still, he had a point and he made it beautifully.

So I'm gonna wear this dress
till the white flies,
give my love to the railroad
till the rain passes me by,
keep twisting my hips
till I hear the sound of eyes looking up
without needing them to look upon me kindly.

Then I'll know that devil was an angel.
And you? You were love.
The real deal, just like I suspected.

Delayed Gratification

I feel middle class when I'm in love.
I think it's all the poached eggs on bird-seed bread,
staying up all night on Zoopla – imagine
waking under cottage beams, the laughter
in a garden. Kids.
A little boy with mixed gold hair
keeps standing in my dreams.

I read somewhere that it takes three hundred years,
about thirteen generations, to change your social class.
I think about this whilst having a fag-I'm-quitting,
head against the doorbell – it's broken
but sometimes after he's left for work,
after the sleepover on the floor beside my single bed,
after a hand-held shower and a pee
in the gaffer-taped loo, I hear it
ringing and ringing.

The shop stewards were taking the necklaces

off the velvet necks
in the jewellery shop windows.

The postage stamp with a bird on
that was in the drawer
had already begun to forget
about its flight via airmail.

We examined each other
carefully, like customs control
or a doctor looking for vulnerable spots:
'Does this hurt? And here?'

My caresses were gloves
I could touch you with:
'Is this good? And here?'

After we slept naked together,
we got dressed again,
but the love still stayed inside us

like when they put stitches on a wound,
but the pain remains.

TRANSLATED BY JAYDE WILL

Bathing Jesse James

I do it on the back porch.
He fills it up. Always on a Wednesday.
It's a quiet day. No one passing

to admire the curling hair on each bare haunch,
the apple at his throat exposed, or yesterday's
bullet holes like white petals blown onto his skin.

I swear his scent's like milk from a stalk
cut from dandelion, or waving prairie daisy.
My husband is a clean man.

He sings, *You are my swaying ear of corn*
as I straighten and lean to sponge him again.
I let my yellow hair swing

to tickle his knees as I kiss him upside-down
where molars glint, crowned with gold. Some say
he stole the lives of seventeen strong men.

I soap each toe, the crooked ankle broken by a horse.
Windstorm's coming. Feel it in my bones. Sideways
he looks at me, then blinks, like looking at the sun.

Waylay of a Lifetime

After Julia Copus

Sure as an oar gestured through water
makes waves, so too is love a rippling
affair that blooms on impact
and leaves a widening wound,
but it's always excusable, a forgivable
vandal. Love's a rustler, most wanted
bushwhacker, the tall hatted stranger
at the steam packet's prow,
and you can be whoever – luthier,
broomsquire, clodhopper, wing walker,
pop up Boulanger – wearing a pastel
sweater the very shade of musk mallow,
throwing in your stake at faro
or in the butterfly house watching pupae
grow and you feel those opening notes,
how love soars to an opus. Yes,
it's bedfellows with footle and bile,
but it's worth every risk and act
of brinkmanship, though it can fray
your moorings and leave you rived to bits.
So c'mon, feverfew lips, you recognise this,
from the daily rushes of your regrets,
the dances you assented to then nixed.

In Palermo With Insomnia

Three days I haven't slept. I see islands on the wall.
Don't you think mafiosi are running our hotel?
You don't. You say a colony of parrots has escaped
and lives unrestrained in the Botanical Gardens.
You want me to see the greenhouse, papayas, rare orchids,
carnivorous plants and ferns that cure liver disease.

You say I'm acting under outdated information –
it's been years and years since Sicily stopped swarming with crime.
So we walk down Via Lincoln. Yes, the light is bronze and fading,
and yes, you were right about these gardens. I give in.
You take me toward a banyan tree, its roots in the air,
and you say, Look what it decided not to bury anymore.

Making Way

A keeper, you said of the house, but I'd sensed everything
trying to make its way: those errant velvet fingers
from your orchid pots; the oak
putting on its chainmail of ivy and moss
and losing; the birds we fed still pinned
to their shadows; crisp wasps
electrocuted by views
through grubby double glazing; and you
just weeks before, showing your wrists
as if uncuffed, asking for my thoughts on a fragrance.

Adjustment

Come the apocalypse
and days of cellars
filled with the very
worst kinds of meat,
you and I, with our scant
supply of practical skills,

will have to rely on these
healing hands of yours.
Oh I know you're bored but
place them again over my
aching spine, feel the discs
shift and realign.

There will be gifts
and furs in tribute, of this
I'm sure. And probably
usurping girls to boot,
who I suppose I'll just
have to learn to kill.

It's difficult for children to pinpoint the exact moment they realise that nothing lasts forever, but rather it slides into view, like the silver wink of the sea as the family Astra rounds the bend of a Lincolnshire hill

Of course I wasn't to know
as Jason Leathen and I
pretended at playing snooker
on a full size table
as dad shuffled Clare and me
round the go-kart track
if only to get our money's worth
as grey day turned to grey night
and the adults all drank
and nobody thought to lament
the fact that the mums and dads
of Netherfield Colts FC (under 15s)
couldn't afford to go abroad
as our static caravan
terrestrial telly
chicken nugget weekend
trundled on like

a 70s fairground ride
that no one found exciting even then
as Butlins spluttered into Monday

of course I wasn't to know
that you were setting yourself on fire
letting yourself love him
for the first time

You probably had brunch
probably held hands
linked   kissed
with February lips
like a torn calendar

I wasn't to know
that one day this would find itself
in a happy poem

breathe out ghosts

I think

I think,
I know,
I am almost completely sure:
he loves me thanks to the mosquitoes,
because when we lie down naked
in the first cool morning breeze
they come and bite
me only,
never him,
him never ever,
so itching my entire body
I scratch till it starts to bleed
and when I wake up my left cheek is swollen
from their poison,
and he only smiles,
because he
doesn't have one blemish
from the blood wedding last night
or the mosquitoes buzzing in the darkness,
who come and bite
me only
never him
him never
ever

TRANSLATED BY JAYDE WILL

Catareen

She's keeping it down next door.
I never have to strain to hear. Far from it.
Normally everything about her

is too much. If she left, I must admit I'd miss
the boyfriend. The best thing about her
is him

trying to holler her name, Catherine,
the French way, *Catarrrreen…* and it's like a moped
hurtling off a cliff, catareening

off a stone face. He can't do it.
But the way he whimpers her name,
after tonight's fight, doesn't tickle at all

like what I'd have picked up in this cup
I slid and held on the wall, pretending to the kids
I was taking out a spider.

Small Lightnings

Driving the A4 to Burghclere, last summer
passes me in an ambulance

on the opposite side. The flashing lights
tell me all I need to know: our time

here is taking its leave on a gurney,
worked at by paramedics whose

urgency is slipping with each
failed shock. I do as Dave says

and stand clear. In doing so I see
she looks very much like you

as you slept through your fever,
those three December days in my room.

When you finally came to, you smiled
and pulled me on top of you. Though now,

it's not looking so good for last summer.
I glimpse your tattoo on her shoulder

as he bends over to massage
the pale ribcage. This year

there is no give back of lightning.
Dave, I say, *we're losing her.*

A Romance

Have you a romance? my mother'd ask,
floury-nosed and teeming in the kitchen
each time I visited,
part apprehensive, part resigned, part hopeful,
her red hands busy building up a dinner.

I have a man, I'd say.
She'd nod, discouraged,
knowing that meant regular sex,
not love and marriage.
My parents remarked,
You've more than we've had hot dinners.

Then there was Dan.
I whispered to her, *I love him,*
and she scrunched my face on her shoulder
in hummocks of woolly.
My eyelids bred stars,
my stomach crimped and curlewed.

I kept it secret, when he left, for weeks.
When I made the announcement, she said,
Do you still want dinner?
She's never asked me since
if I've a romance.

Beverage Out The Boy

Drown the boy in coffee,
stick a biscuit in his mouth. Let questions crumb
and sweep away on a tongue of river,
a flush of sun. Leave the house with a stack
of books and breathe out ghosts,
sunset yellows the castle and crossing
the bridge you love the river's swerve
and dip, cobbles kicking your feet. Stop
for coffee, coffee carries you
through late night library trips, now sip
and flick fingers over book spines,
cool and curving out to touch. Not the dip
of his back, the mattress sink,
warmth electric sweet as mocha. Press skin
to flushed polystyrene, Euripides' *Medea*.
Blip your books, swipe your pass and stop
for coffee, your lips were meant
for its plastic kiss. See the rowers master
the will of the river, how in the light its surface
is spilt glitter, the castle lit up like a carousel.
Drown the boy in river and sun and the flush of light
on cobbles. Stack his back with books,
stuff Sophocles in his mouth. Sweep crumbs
from the bed, resist the dip and river
of sheets. Drink drink forget.

Small Loss of Every Softness

And when you are out of the room
making your huge coffee
doing your hair or something.

I take your make-up brush
I run it across my face
I dust stuff. I exhale. I inhale.

       'Wait
      there,' and
I write the words *small softness* in my notebook,
'just breathe this perfectly smelling thing,' I say.

*

Listen to Joni Mitchell and the soundtrack
from Juno take long breaks from draft emails
to universities galleries homestays on the WEST

to stare at the jars in the abyss of the fridge
hate my sister for her pickling of things compose
a terse sanctuary in verse, a real achievement

       on the preserving of figs.
turn every lovely photo every lovely photo every lovely photo
there is nothing in tomorrow for I give all days to this

*

It is not that the sky

beyond the window of the train
that that sky is actually naturally bleak

ever. What is that? Where
would be the bleak in nature?
Just the trees are helpless

fingerprints along the horizon.
fuck this. then, *fuck writing poems*
The woman across from me is sleeping.

She used to be my sweetheart.
She used to be my best friend.
I am in love with this stranger.

I wonder if I tell her
I am about to Ophelia myself
right here

whether maybe she could halve me
her Roast Chicken sandwich,
agree to kick me lightly

take me back and let me sip her simply
roll her coffee awful eyes at me

*

Spring continues.
The past perfect Summer flattens.
And now this

looking at my fingers. Just that
when we finally collide
you say vague things

about life being in passing
wrapped up in cling-film
and it echoes in my own petulance.

I must leave this city. This tragedy
of particulars. Our cling-film visions
unjoin their similar distants.

And so I give it all to my notebook
all scent, all exactness.   *all excellence*
the small of every softness,   *gone*

JODY PORTER

Not the Wallpaper Game

After 'Not the Furniture Game' by Simon Armitage

Her hair was a belle époque motif
and her eyes were the shipwrecks of all of her lovers
and her cheeks were the intricate tools of goldsmiths
and her teeth were a taxonomy of gems and their hardnesses
and her bite was a sister's lifesaving transfusion
and her nostrils were solemn funeral horses
and her mouth was a heroin death in Montmartre
and her smile was a rifle kept loaded in readiness
and her tongue was the arches of Chartres Cathedral
and her whistle was a neighbour's impeccable garden
and her laugh was a murmuration of starlings.
She coughed, and it was privatisation.
And her headaches were monstrous glacial decouplings
and her arguments were cats always landing feet-down
and her neck was a pietà illuminated with grief
and her throat was a landmine grown over with roses
and her arms were the antidote to the sufferings of war
and her elbows were the frictionless hinges of a vault
and her wrists were the ribbons being saved for Christmas
and her handshakes were deer tracks in unseasonable snow
and her fingers were holidaymakers fresh from the plane
and the palms of her hands were the deserts of martyrdom
and her thumbs were the small-hour muddling of cocktails.
She had a thin black cat, it was named Dolce Vita.
Her shadow was an astrolabe
and her heart was a universe

and her shoulder blades were the deathly roosting of hawks
and her belly button was her mother
and her sex was a weapon
and her back was a protest
and her hips were a pin-up.
The whole system of her blood was a dragonfly's wing.
And her legs were an heiress
and her knees were the first soft conkers of autumn
and her ligaments were a heist movie
and her calves were oysters.
The balls of her feet were lightning conductors
and her toes were flower buds closed in the night.
And her footprints were raindrops
and her promises were blood money
and her one-liners were sonnets
and her goodbyes were the tremblings of the world on its axis
and the last time we spoke, it was an extravagant snowfight.

She forever recurred, like a detail in chinoiserie wallpaper –
a bird perhaps, or bamboo.

And now whenever I see you
you're a lengthening list of things I wish I'd said
and here it is.

NASHWA GOWANLOCK

The Book Of Coming Forth By Day

I could tell you about my plants, all dried up
and how I don't know whether to believe
in plant biology, and wait until spring,
watering them faithfully like the old woman
who force-fed her husband long after he died.
And how can we know when something has truly
ceased. Let me be that old woman feeding my man
through his passage to the eternal rest, holding
on to his hand, pressing my forehead
against his, feeling how that calms his mind.
When he wakes, sitting with his back to the door,
cross-legged and rocking gently with each short
intake of breath, perhaps he'll be waiting for me
to stop, just a breadth of a river out of reach.

In The Way

What are you doing here?
You are in the wrong place.
You should be filling the space
between the sink and me when I want to rinse my mug.
You should be in front of that drawer
whenever I need to open it,
hips against it as you chop the veg,
and opening the dishwasher door
so I need to step over it to get to the fridge.
You should be filling the kettle
just as I reach for it,
my hand suspended in the air.
You should be using the tea towel
so I end up drying my hands on your back.
You should not be tucked away,
here under your tree.
Darling, you should always be in the way.

Chorister, St Saviour's Church, Southwark, 1607

I aim my voice at the vaults,
my truest notes, with all
the sweetness I can muster –

balm to his buboes,
calm to his fever,
unction in his resting place.

This afternoon, across the bridge,
I must exchange my surplice
for Titania's gown.

He used to be my Oberon;
each day he stroked my cheek.
I could load my eyes into his

and let my heart speak
through his brother's words.
His lips were mink on mine.

What's left? This smell
from seventy smouldering wicks,
a rare forenoon toll,

the sight of his tomb shining
from the choir floor
for as long as I can sing?

I'll dress in foolish columbine
and strip a songbird's wing.

The Commiphora Myrrh Tree

for P. H., First British Heart Foundation Professor of Cardiology

They wound the trees for their resin,
it's a well-known fact and him, dead.

Up the stairs to sleep she thinks about him –
deceased, rubbed out.

And she is wounded like the trees
they bleed for resin.

He, twenty years her senior, so at ease in the world,
why leave it so suddenly?

She wonders did he lose direction from his lab
into the mortuary and then not know how to exit

and what about all that he'd pioneered, those paintings,
his violin, all that work on the heart, all aspirations

over-ruled as he was left on a cold slab,
in a busy hospital, an unremarkable day, his own autopsy.

He'd never told her if he'd seen the resin collected
for this myrrh, his present from Jerusalem.

She'd always meant to ask and now the crystals sit
on the kitchen table. He'd taught her trees are wounded.

Atrial Fibrillation, he'd teased over dinner one night,
would never enter a poem

but for her a strain lingers around these words,
a quest for further knowledge.

An unremarkable day, his own autopsy.
There must be a way to stop the trees from bleeding.

KATHLEEN MORAN BAINBRIDGE

Holdfast

You hold my cigarette, you fold your hand
into mine, you lay a palm on the old cat's head
to say goodbye, you spend half a lifetime

losing your way and your keys, when you cut bread
I have to hide my eyes. You wonder aloud
at the roll of a batsman's wrist, the fine rain

of *Misty*'s glissando shimmy. My gold band
stays on your fingerbone under the ground.
I see you wave to me often, cheering me on.

Let's both

A Cardiogram

It starts with a steep learning curve:
we're discovering each other – the shapes of our faces
and more intimate parts, the feel of our words. Hang up.
No, *you* hang up. No, *you* hang up. No, *you*.

But the heart is a strategic dealer, feeding many
a loss-leader in those early days. Things peak, usually
on a Sunday morning in August – in bare feet and light
cotton, over coffee and croissants and breakfast-time sex.

By evening we sense precipice, tomorrow
is a work day and we can't agree. I want to go for a walk,
I have visions of philosophy and sunset. You dress in sweatpants
to watch costume drama on the BBC, just after the watershed.

Which is fitting as it is at this point we start to drain
into a different valley. Steep, littered with scree: your stupid hair,
my eating too fast, just the sound of you breathing. Fuck off.
No, *you* fuck off. No, *you* fuck off. No, *you*.

A sudden thud – we've not given up.
Give us credit, we're making an effort here! Hauling
the weight of each other back into light. Recovering love.
Heaving back the tarps – rediscovering.

Into that second, lesser peak with its trailing
undulations: a trip to the city for birthday gifts; a meal out
without the kids. Occasionally *Smells Like Teen Spirit* gatecrashes
Radio 2. Shifting the Volvo into sixth on the A47.

And all this 60 to 100 times a minute. Now,
I'm no cardiologist, I just own a heart. I'm no physicist
but I know something about the ambition of forces. Hold on.
No, *you* hold on. No, *you* hold on. Let's both.

Symbiosis

The Egyptian plover takes for his lover
the Nile crocodile. An unlikely pairing,
feathers with scales, finicking wade with
splayed legs, but she welcomes him wet-eyed
and wide-jawed. He hops within and tenderly
plucks leeches from her gums, so light on her
tongue that each deft step is barely felt
as surviving shifts into caress.

He knows from observation the snap
of tessellating maw round prey,
and once saw his love rip shreds from a giraffe;
when he waded out the river ran red.
But they share four-chambered hearts which beat in time
and he eats at the table of her smile.

Love Parade

The heartthrobs ferrying Miss Universe
on a lacquered palanquin fly streamers

from their naked shoulders,

and blow their kisses also to the crowds.
Between the penthouse balconies

noon burnishes a fleet of cartoon giants

filled with helium, pours
ponds of shade over the puppeteers

who soak below like fishing lures.

The marching bands have drunk
such pleasure, they're spewing

confetti wherever they go.

Baton twirlers on roller skates.
Floats dressed in live butterflies.

And while saints-to-be throw chocolates

from the backs of pachyderms,
I roll around the corner

in the car we first kissed in.

The paintjob's a roaring canary
and that's pink champagne in my hand.

Kiss/Kiss

Love comes around again, hot pulse in the chest,
so unexpected, so familiar. You pull up a chair
and when we kiss the way we've always kissed

but deeper, all the years of reckoning pressed
between our lips, drifts of old songs in the air,
love comes around again, hot pulse in the chest,

long love, love's work. Who would have guessed
we'd still be here bending time, with time to spare?
And when we kiss the way we've always kissed,

it's like the first kiss. It was raining. I was pissed,
you were surprised; what was it? We didn't care.
Love comes around again, hot pulse in the chest.

Perhaps we knew more wonder then, but now is best:
the old wounds ache and yet we still go there
though when we kiss the way we've always kissed

sometimes it hurts. This kiss comes with a twist:
these wounds we made, each time we kiss them better
love comes around again, hot pulse in the chest.
Let's kiss, my love, the way we always kissed.

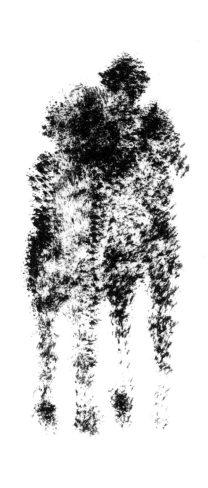

ACKNOWLEDGEMENTS

'Love Parade' by George David Clark was first published in *Southern Poetry Review* (2013).

'A Romance' by Kitty Coles was first published in *Mslexia,* Issue 18 (2003).

'Dear Lab-Man' by Ellie Danak was first published in *Magma* 68, 'Margins'.

'Louder Than Words' by Alexandra Davis was first published in *Awakening* (2015), an anthology by the Felixstowe Café Poets.

'The Record Player' by Frank Dullaghan was previously published in his collection *Enough Light to See the Dark* (Cinnamon Press, 2011).

'Chorister, St Saviour's Church, Southwark, 1607' by Chrissie Gittins was first published in her collection *I'll Dress One Night as You* (Salt, 2009). Note: Edmund Shakespeare, William's youngest brother and an actor, died aged 27. He is buried in St Saviour's Church – now Southwark Cathedral.

'Yes' by Ramona Herdman was first published in *The Interpreter's House* (2015).

'Letter composed to Genghis Khan in my head (whilst in bed)' by Jack Houston was first published in *The Interpreter's House.*

'Bathing Jesse James' by Anna Kisby was first published in *Mslexia*, Issue 43 (2009).

'Beverage Out The Boy' by Rowena Knight was first published on Pomegranate Poetry.

'Larder' by Gill Learner has previously appeared on the BBC Radio 3 website for their 2007 Valentine's Day competition, in *Cracking On: poems on ageing by older women,* ed. Joy Howard (Grey Hen Press, 2009) and in her collection *The Agister's Experiment* (Two Rivers Press, 2011).

'Delayed Gratification' by Rachel Long was published in *Whisper the Wrong Name* (Jerwood/Arvon Anthology Vol. Six, 2016) and *The Honest Ulsterman* (2016).

'Small Lightnings' by Martin Malone was first published in his collection *Cur* (Shoestring, 2015).

'The Harvest' by Abigail Meeke was first published by Write Out Loud (2017).

'My First Husband' by Marie Naughton was previously published by *Southword Journal* 28 (2015) and *The Irish Examiner* (September 2015).

'Small Loss of Every Softness' by Penny Newell was first published in *The Still Point Journal*, Issue 2 (2017).

'Note from Edinburgh' by Stav Poleg was first published in *South Bank Poetry*, Issue 19 (2014).

'Postscript' by Kate Potts was first published by Visual Verse in 2016.

'The Noonday Devil' by Shauna Robertson was first published in *Ambit* 212 (2013).

'Kiss/Kiss' by Jacqueline Saphra was first published in her collection *All My Mad Mothers* (Nine Arches, 2017).

'Romantic' by Stephen Sexton was first published in *Winter Papers* 3 (2017).

'sorry (i forgot your Unbirthday) e e' by James Walton was first published in *Little Raven Anthology of Erotic Literature* (2016).

'Adjustment' by Ruth Wiggins was first published in her pamphlet *Myrtle* (Emma Press, 2014).

ABOUT THE EDITORS

Rachel Piercey is a poet and editor for adults and children. She regularly performs her poems and runs writing workshops at schools and festivals across the country. Rachel's poems have appeared in *The Rialto, Magma, Poems in Which, Butcher's Dog* and *The Poetry Review*, as well as various Emma Press pamphlets and anthologies, and in 2008 she won the Newdigate Prize. She lives in London.

Emma Wright worked in ebook production at Orion Publishing Group before leaving to found the Emma Press in 2012 with the support of the Prince's Trust Explore Enterprise programme. She lives in Birmingham.

ABOUT THE AUTHORS

Catherine Ayres is a teacher from Northumberland. Her poems have appeared in a number of magazines, including *Mslexia* and *The Moth*. In 2015 she came third in the Hippocrates Prize and in 2016 she won the Elbow Room Prize. Her debut collection is *Amazon* (Indigo Dreams, 2016).

Kathleen Moran Bainbridge has worked as a singer, teacher and Gestalt therapist. In 2014 she was runner-up for the Flambard Prize and in 2015 she won a New Writing North award. Her poems have appeared in magazines, anthologies and online. She lives across a ford in Northumberland.

Daisy Behagg won the Bridport Prize for poetry 2013. She has been widely published in journals including *The Poetry Review, The Morning Star, Poetry Wales, Ambit* and *Poems in Which*. She is a student mental health nurse and lives in Brighton.

Carole Bromley lives in York. She has two collections with Smith/Doorstop: *A Guided Tour of the Ice House* and *The Stonegate Devil,* which won the 2016 York Culture Award. Her first collection of poems for children, *Blast Off!,* was published in June 2017.

Jane Burn is originally from South Yorkshire and is now based in the North East. Her poems have been published in magazines including *The Rialto* and *Under the Radar.* Her first collection, *nothing more to it than bubbles,* has been published by Indigo Dreams.

Jared A. Carnie lives in Sheffield. He won a Northern Writers' Award in 2015 and his debut novel, *Waves,* is available now.

George David Clark's *Reveille* won the Miller Williams Prize and his more recent work can be found in *AGNI, The Georgia Review, The Gettysburg Review, The Southern Review* and elsewhere. He edits *32 Poems* and lives with his wife and their three young children in Washington, Pennsylvania.

Kitty Coles' poems have been widely published in magazines and anthologies. She is one of the two winners of the Indigo Dreams Pamphlet Prize 2016 and her debut pamphlet, *Seal Wife,* was published in 2017. www.kittyrcoles.com

Ellie Danak has a background in researching Swedish crime novels. Her work has been featured in Emma Press and Paper Swans Press anthologies and in a wide range of magazines.

Alexandra Davis is an English teacher living in Suffolk with her husband and four sons. Her debut pamphlet, *Sprouts,* was published in August 2017 by Dempsey & Windle. Her poems have been published in *Agenda, Artemis* and Emma Press anthologies. www.alexandrapoet.wordpress.com

Frank Dullaghan is an Irish writer living in Dubai. He has three collections published by Cinnamon Press, the most recent being *The Same Roads Back* (2014). In 2016 he had a pamphlet, *Secrets of the Body*, published by Eyewear Press. He is published widely in UK and Irish journals.

Wendy French has four full collections of poetry published and won the Hippocrates Poetry and Medicine prize for the NHS section in 2010. She facilitates creative writing in healthcare settings. She was poet-in-residence at the University College Hospital Macmillan Cancer Centre in 2015.

Chrissie Gittins has two poetry collections for adults: *Armature* (Arc, 2003) and *I'll Dress One Night as You* (Salt, 2009). Her latest children's collection featured on BBC Countryfile. She visits schools, and has read at the Hay, Edinburgh, West Cork and Shetland festivals. www.chrissiegittins.co.uk

Nashwa Gowanlock is a writer, journalist, and literary translator with an MFA in writing from the Vermont College of Fine Arts. She has translated numerous works of Arabic literature, including poems by Moroccan poet Mohammed Bennis and a co-translation of Samar Yazbek's memoir, *The Crossing: My Journey to the Shattered Heart of Syria*.

Caroline Hardaker lives in Newcastle upon Tyne with her husband, a giant cat, and a forest of houseplants. Her poetry has been published widely, most recently or forthcoming in *Magma, Neon* and *Shoreline of Infinity*. Her debut chapbook, *Bone Ovation,* was published by Valley Press in 2017.

Ramona Herdman's pamphlet *Bottle* is available from HappenStance Press and is the Poetry Book Society Pamphlet Choice for Spring 2018. She won The Poetry Society's Hamish Canham prize 2017. She lives in Norwich and is a committee member for Café Writers.

Lizzie Holden is a London poet. She finds her poems are primarily about love and loss. The themes of abuse, dance, trees and breath also find their way into poem shaped forms. Some of her poems are tiny. Her work has been published by Pankhearst Press, Picaroon Poetry and Sable Books.

Jack Houston lives in London with his wife and son, plays drums with his band, Bugeye, and is a founding member of a radical housing coop. He works in Hackney's Libraries, where he regularly runs free poetry workshops. His work has featured in *Brittle Star, Magma* and *Butcher's Dog.*

Paul Howarth was born in Chester and now lives in Suffolk with his wife and two boys. He is a writer and a photographer and he works promoting reading through libraries and beyond. Most recently he has poems published by the Emma Press and in *Under the Radar.*

Anna Kisby is a Devon-based poet, widely published in magazines and anthologies. She won the BBC Proms Poetry Competition 2016 and was commended in the Faber New Poets Scheme 2015-16. Her debut pamphlet *All the Naked Daughters* is published by Against the Grain Press (2017).

Rowena Knight grew up in New Zealand and splits her time between Bristol and London. Her poems have appeared in various magazines including *Bare Fiction, Butcher's Dog, Magma,* and *The Rialto.* Her first pamphlet, *All the Footprints I Left Were Red,* was published by Valley Press in 2016.

Anja Konig grew up in the German language and now writes in English. Her first pamphlet, *Advice for an Only Child,* was shortlisted for the 2015 Michael Marks Award.

Gill Learner married Trevor in London 56 years ago; they now live in Reading. She has won several prizes, including The Poetry Society's Hamish Canham award, and been published widely. She has two collections with Two Rivers Press: *The Agister's Experiment* (2011) and *Chill Factor* (2016).

Rachel Long was awarded a Jerwood/Arvon mentorship in 2015. She is assistant tutor to Jacob Sam-La Rose on the Barbican Young Poets programme, and leader of Octavia, a poetry collective for women of colour, which is housed at Southbank Centre.

Anne Macaulay was born in rural, northern Scotland but, after meeting her husband in the 70s, has embraced urban life in East London. Since retiring from teaching and her children growing up, poetry has become her focus. She has had poems published in several anthologies, and enjoys poetry classes and performing poetry.

Antony Mair lives in Hastings. He has had poems accepted for publication in numerous magazines and several anthologies. He won first prize in the Rottingdean Writers National Poetry Competition 2016 and was shortlisted in the Live Canon Poetry Competitions 2016 and 2017.

Martin Malone was born in County Durham and now lives in Scotland. He has published two poetry collections: *The Waiting Hillside* (Templar, 2011) and *Cur* (Shoestring, 2015). His third collection, *The Unreturning*, is forthcoming. He edits *The Interpreter's House* poetry journal.

Roy McFarlane was born in Birmingham. He is of Jamaican parentage and has been Birmingham's Poet Laureate. Roy co-edited *Celebrate Wha?* (Smokestack, 2011) and his first poetry collection, *Beginning With Your Last Breath*, was published by Nine Arches Press (2016).

Abigail Meeke is a journalist with a BA in Theology and an MA in Creative Writing. She was born and bred in West Wales but now lives in Devon with her husband and their two young daughters, Beatrice and Alexandra.

Rob Miles lives in Yorkshire. His poetry appears widely in magazines and anthologies. He has won the Philip Larkin

Prize, judged by Don Paterson, and the Resurgence Prize, judged by Jo Shapcott and Imtiaz Dharker.

Cynthia Miller is a Malaysian-American poet and brand strategist. Her poems have been published in *Primers Volume 2, Butcher's Dog* and *Under the Radar* and shortlisted for the Bridport Poetry Prize. She is also co-director of Verve, a Birmingham Festival of Poetry and Spoken Word.

Marie Naughton's poems have appeared widely in magazines and anthologies. She won the Café Writers competition in 2012 and was awarded second prize in *Mslexia*'s competition in 2016. Her first collection is forthcoming in 2018 from Pindrop Press.

Penny Newell has a PhD from King's College London and is a Reader at Frontier Poetry. Her writing has featured in the *TLS, The Cardiff Review, The Still Point Journal* and *Alien Mouth*, and is forthcoming in *The Portland Review* and *3:AM*. She is currently commissioned for Lakes Ignite 2018.

Ben Norris is a poet, playwright, and actor, and two-time national poetry slam champion. His debut solo show, *The Hitchhiker's Guide to the Family*, won the IdeasTap Underbelly Award, and his first short film, produced by Channel 4, was nominated for a Royal Television Society Award.

Paulius Norvila graduated with an MA in Economics from Vilnius University in 2009. Since 2004 he has published both poetry and prose. He is the author of three poetry collections, *The Seven Seasons* (2006), *Drawing the Cards is Just a Part of the Ritual* (2012), and *The Everyday* (2014).

Tish Oakwood has been addicted to words since she was a child, smuggling a torch, Scrabble board and dictionary under the bedclothes. Since then she has been published in various magazines and anthologies, and placed in competitions. Tish teaches occasional poetry workshops and short courses.

Richard O'Brien's pamphlets include *The Emmores* (Emma Press, 2014) and *A Bloody Mess* (Valley Press, 2015). His work has featured in *Oxford Poetry, Poetry London*, and *The Salt Book of Younger Poets*. His first children's play was produced at the Arcola Theatre in December 2016.

Catherine Olver is a Cambridge-based poet who loves to rhyme. Her doctoral research considers representations of the five senses in contemporary YA fantasy novels. Catherine holds an MA in Place & Environment Writing from Royal Holloway and was a Foyle Young Poet in 2010.

Eeva Park was born into a writers' family in 1950 in Tallinn, Estonia. She made her debut with a poetry collection, *Mõrkjas tuul* (Acrid Wind, 1983), and has published a total of seven poetry collections to date, along with several award-winning novels, short stories and radio plays.

Maya Pieris has had poems published widely, including in *South Poetry,* and one of her play scripts won a Page to Stage Tacchi-Morris Award. Maya recently received third prize in a Jane Austen-inspired competition organised by SaveAs Writers and the University of Kent.

Rachel Plummer is a poet who lives in Edinburgh with her partner and two young children. Rachel is a Scottish Book Trust New Writers Award recipient and has recently released a pamphlet of sci-fi poems with House Press, called *The Parlour Guide to Exo-Politics.*

Stav Poleg's poetry has appeared in *The New Yorker, Poetry London,* and *Poetry Ireland Review*. Her graphic-novel installation, *Dear Penelope: Variations on an August Morning*, with artist Laura Gressani, was acquired by the Scottish National Gallery of Modern Art. She lives in Cambridge, UK.

Jody Porter is poetry editor for the *Morning Star*. His work has appeared in *Magma, Best British Poetry 2013* (Salt), *Best*

New British and Irish Poets 2016 (Eyewear) and elsewhere. Originally from Essex, he now lives in London where he is involved in the Stoke Newington Literary Festival.

Kate Potts is a London-based poet and creative writing lecturer. Her first full-length collection is *Pure Hustle* (Bloodaxe). Kate teaches for Oxford University, Royal Holloway, and The Poetry School. She has recently completed a PhD on the poetic radio play.

Samuel Prince lives and works in London. His poems have been published in various print and online magazines, including *Cordite Poetry Review, Magma, Menacing Hedge* and *Poetry Salzburg Review,* as well as the anthologies *Birdbook 2, Coin Opera 2* and *Lives Beyond Us* (all Sidekick Books).

Shauna Robertson's poems have been set to music, displayed on buses, made into comic art, hung on a pub wall, and published in various lit mags and anthologies. She has two chapbooks: *Blueprints for a Minefield* and *Hack*. Shauna also writes for children and makes artwork.

Lenni Sanders is a writer/performer in Manchester, UK. She is the general editor at *Cadaverine Magazine*, and makes interactive performances with Curious Things and absurdist poetry cabaret with Dead Lads. Her writing has appeared in *The Tangerine, Butcher's Dog* and elsewhere. @LenniSanders

Jacqueline Saphra's recent pamphlets are *If I Lay on my Back I Saw Nothing but Naked Women* (Emma Press, 2014) and *A Bargain with the Light: Poems after Lee Miller* (Hercules Editions, 2017). Her latest collection, *All My Mad Mothers* (Nine Arches, 2017), is shortlisted for the T.S. Eliot prize.

Stephen Sexton lives in Belfast. His poems have appeared in *Granta, Poetry London* and *Best British Poetry 2015*, and his pamphlet, *Oils*, published by the Emma Press in 2014, was the Poetry Book Society's Winter Pamphlet Choice. He was the winner of the 2016 National Poetry Competition.

Arvis Viguls is a Latvian poet and translator based in Riga where he lives together with his wife and their cat Žižek. His work includes two award-winning poetry collections in Latvian and a book of selected poems in Spanish translation.

James Walton is an Australian poet published widely in newspapers, journals and anthologies. His work has been shortlisted twice for the ACU National Literature Prize and the MPU International Poetry Prize. His collection *The Leviathan's Apprentice* was published in 2015.

Ruth Wiggins lives in London. Her poems have appeared most recently in *POETRY, The Poetry Review, Long Poem Magazine* and *The Wolf*. Her pamphlet *Myrtle* was published by the Emma Press in 2014 and was runner-up in the Fledgling Poetry Award. She blogs at mudpath.wordpress.com

Rachel Willems is an American poet and fiction writer who grew up in Washington State and studied poetry at the University of Washington and Boston University. Her work has appeared in *The London Magazine, Tahoma Literary Review* and *Streetlight Magazine*.

Jayde Will is a literary translator. He has an MA in Fenno-Ugric Linguistics from Tartu University. His translations of Latvian, Lithuanian, and Estonian authors have been published in numerous journals, including *The Poetry Review, Trafika* and *Mantis*.

Kate Wise fits poetry around two small people and a career in law. She has been published in several Emma Press anthologies, and various journals including *The Rialto, Structo* and *Poems in Which*. She grew up in Cheshire, lives in London, and tweets at @kwise62

Andrew Wynn Owen is an Examination Fellow at All Souls College, Oxford. In 2015, he received an Eric Gregory Award. His first poetry pamphlet, *Raspberries for the Ferry*, was published by the Emma Press in 2014, followed by a collaboration with John Fuller, *AWOL*, in 2015.

ABOUT THE EMMA PRESS

small press, big dreams

☙❧

The Emma Press is an independent publisher dedicated to producing beautiful, thought-provoking books. It was founded in 2012 by Emma Wright in Winnersh and is now based in Birmingham.

Having been shortlisted in both 2014 and 2015, the Emma Press won the Michael Marks Award for Poetry Pamphlet Publishers in 2016.

The Emma Press is passionate about publishing literature which is welcoming and accessible. Sign up to the Emma Press newsletter to hear about upcoming events, publications and calls for submissions.

theemmapress.com
emmavalleypress.blogspot.co.uk

ALSO FROM THE EMMA PRESS

MILDLY EROTIC VERSE

Edited by Rachel Piercey and Emma Wright
RRP £10 / ISBN 978-1-910139-34-9

Mildly Erotic Verse skips the mechanics and dives straight into the emotional core of sex, celebrating the diversity and eccentricity of human sexuality.

POSTCARD STORIES

Stories by Jan Carson, illustrated by Benjamin Phillips
RRP £6.50 / ISBN 978-1-910139-68-4

Every day in 2015, Jan Carson wrote a short story on the back of a postcard and mailed it to a friend. Each of these tiny stories was inspired by an event, an overheard conversation, a piece of art or just a glance of something worth thinking about further.

FIRST FOX

Stories by Leanne Radojkovich, illustrated by Rachel J Fenton
RRP £6.50 / ISBN 978-1-910139-70-7

The stories in *First fox* offer an everyday world tinged with the dreamlike qualities of fairy tales. Disappointments and consolations meet with fantastical moments, winding their way into the realm of possibility.

Now You Can Look

Poems by Julia Bird, illustrated by Anna Vaivare
RRP £10 / ISBN 978-1-910139-84-4

This is a tale you can read three ways. The first time through, it's the story of a woman who takes one glance at conventional early-twentieth-century life, and throws in her lot with art instead.

Dragonish

Poems by Emma Simon, introduced by Caroline Bird
RRP £6.50 / ISBN 978-1-910139-64-6

Loss, love and various severed body parts are scattered throughout *Dragonish*. The poems are rooted in family, friends and home while also reaching into other worlds: the circus of possibilities, an earth-bound heavenly host, London's dryads and a nineteenth-century French brothel.

The Secret Box

Stories by Daina Tabūna, translated by Jayde Will
RRP £6.50 / ISBN 9-78-1-910139-90-5

On the cusp of womanhood, Daina Tabūna's heroines are constantly confronted with the unexpected. Adult life seems just around the corner, but so are the kinds of surprise encounter which might change everything.

ALSO FROM THE EMMA PRESS

Paisley

Poems by Rakhshan Rizwan, introduced by Leila Aboulela
RRP £6.50 / ISBN 978-1-910139-78-3

Drawing on the rich visual and material culture of her home region, Rizwan unpacks and offers critical comment on the vexed issues of class, linguistic and cultural identity – particularly for women – in the context of Pakistan and South Asia.

The Emma Press Anthology of Aunts

Edited by Rachel Piercey and Emma Wright
RRP £10 / ISBN 978-1-910139-66-0

The *Anthology of Aunts* explores what it means to be – and feels like to have – an aunt, historically and today. Some aunts are biological, some are chosen, but all have an impact on the way we learn to move through the world.

The Emma Press Anthology of the Sea

Edited by Eve Lacey
RRP £10 / ISBN 978-1-910139-45-5

In the *Anthology of the Sea*, poets ask how the human mind can fathom the ocean's depths. The sea emerges as at once strange and familiar, bearing witness to storms, ocean creatures and the human desire for freedom.

GOOSE FAIR NIGHT

Poems by Kathy Pimlott, introduced by Clare Pollard
RRP £6.50 / ISBN 978-1-910139-35-6

Goose Fair Night is a generous, jellied feast of a book, full of sharp-eyed yet tender details about friendship, family and familiarity. The poems plunge us into the Midlands, bustling central London, seaside scenes, questionable pots of jam, and the captivating worldview of Pimlott's grandmother Enid.

THE EMMA PRESS ANTHOLOGY OF MOTHERHOOD

Edited by Rachel Piercey and Emma Wright
RRP £10 / ISBN 978-0-9574596-7-0

An anthology which celebrates and examines the complexity of emotion surrounding motherhood. The darkest thoughts of exhausted mothers are sensitively portrayed, as poets expose the weight of responsibility behind the state of motherhood, and question the expectations society places on mothers.